Christmas
WREATHS &
CENTERPIECES

Christmas WREATHS & CENTERPIECES

How to Create, Design, and Make Them

Margaret Grace

Weidenfeld & Nicolson
New York

A TERN BOOK

Copyright © 1987 by Tern Enterprises Inc.

Published by Weidenfeld & Nicolson, New York
A Division of Wheatland Corporation
10 East 53rd Street
New York, New York 10022

Library of Congress Cataloging-in-Publication Data

Christmas wreaths and centerpieces.

1. Wreaths. 2. Flower arrangement. 3. Christmas
decorations. 4. Table setting and decoration.
I. Weidenfeld and Nicolson (Firm)
SB449.5.W74C48   1987   745.92'6   87-8246
ISBN 1-55584-135-X

CHRISTMAS WREATHS AND CENTERPIECES
How to Create, Design, and Make Them
was prepared and produced by
Tern Enterprises Inc.
15 West 26th Street
New York, New York 10010

Editor: Louise Quayle
Art Director: Mary Moriarty
Designer: Liz Trovato
Photo Editor: Philip Hawthorne
Production Manager: Karen L. Greenberg

Typeset by BPE Graphics, Inc.
Color separations by Hong Kong Scanner Craft Company Ltd.
Printed and bound in Hong Kong by Leefung Asco Printers Ltd.

First Edition 1987

10 9 8 7 6 5 4 3 2 1

To Rod, David, and Hattie
whose mutual cooperation makes everything better

CHRISTMAS WREATHS

Introduction
page 8

The Art of Wreathmaking
page 10

Evergreen Wreaths
page 12

Vine, Everlasting, and Cone Wreaths
page 28

Novelty Wreaths
page 44

CHRISTMAS
CENTERPIECES

Introduction
page 54

Begin at the Beginning
page 56

Flowers, Greens, and Fruit
page 58

Setting a Christmas Stage
page 66

8

CHRISTMAS WREATHS

Like no other time of the year, the Christmas season allows tremendous opportunities for expression through decoration. There can never be too much attention paid to decorative detail: flourishes of greens, flowers, ribbons, and multitudes of sparkling lights look wonderful now. At the same time, the seasonal starkness of Christmastime in many parts of the country gives even the lightest decorative touches a special focus and appeal. Wreaths and centerpieces are marvelous embellishments for the holiday home. They are decorative touches for interior spaces—mantelpieces, over buffets, in entry halls—so the designs you can create are virtually limitless. Both make very special and enduring gifts, particularly when hand-fashioned with your individualized style and affection for the recipient.

9

The Art of Wreathmaking

The festive spirit of Christmas begins at the front door with a beautiful wreath. In ancient Rome, wreaths were symbols of victory and celebration. Today, their celebratory symbolism has also come to connote continuity and tradition.

The wreaths described in this book are divided into three types—evergreen; vine, everlasting, and cone; and novelty wreaths. Choose for your family and friends wreaths that suit their taste and style in the bases, size, and adornments they prefer.

Robert Gray

Evergreen Wreaths

Evergreen is the most commonly used base for holiday wreaths. A red-sashed wreath gracing the front door has a simple, timeless beauty that heralds the Christmas season. Fashioned of boughs of pine and spruce, evergreen wreaths, which range in size from 8 to 24 inches, are widely available through nurseries and florists. The density and color of these purchased wreaths can be enhanced easily by inserting short sprigs of holly or boxwood into the branches of the wreath. Evergreen wreaths, generally fastened together with wire, will support all sorts of adornments in their branches without additional fasteners. An exception are pinecones—a favorite decoration for their natural, rustic beauty. These must be secured to the wreath with a small piece of florist wire, which is twisted around the base of the cone, then anchored to the wreath.

EVERGREEN WREATHS

CHRISTMAS WREATHS

Robert Gray

David Arky

The addition of small red bows, tied at the cone bases before they are wired to the wreath, is a simple, effective flourish on this evergreen wreath.

Bamboo roping, wrapped all around the wreath is an unusual touch. Add straw or wooden ornaments and wide plaid bows, which you can tie directly to the wreath, to create a full, highly textured, country look.

Robert Gray

An interesting, elaborate variation on a country look is this evergreen wreath that is trimmed with an inner circle of looped, dried corn husks and country-look fabric. The individual sheaths of corn husk and fabric are cut to equal size— approximately 4 by 8 inches. The rectangles are separately folded over so that the narrow ends meet, taking care not to crease the center bend. The joined ends of the rectangle are then gathered tightly and wrapped around with fine florist wire. They are then individually wired to the evergreen wreath, alternating husk and fabric as illustrated. Finally, the wreath is topped with a plaid fabric bow.

David Arky

A lush, reckless wreath for the musician on your list is pictured here. Fistfulls of dried baby's breath are inserted into a full evergreen wreath. Dried, parchment-colored hydrangea blossoms arc placed among the branches along with pages of sheet music that have been fan-folded. A long string of gold-bead roping keeps the elements in place with a gilt touch.

Robert Gray

The addition of starfish, attached directly to the branches of this wreath with white glue, makes a witty, personal statement about the designer. The lush velvet bow, twice looped and tied to the top of the wreath, adds elegance.

All of these evergreen wreaths will wear better and last longer if gently misted daily with cool water. Take special care, too, to fasten them securely to their posts to prevent too much movement when doors are opened and closed.

EVERGREEN WREATHS

Boxwood is a lovely bush of evergreen habit. It is often used by nurseries to create holiday roping. That roping, tightly wound around itself and secured with wire, makes a charming, dense, shiny-leafed wreath. Clusters of artificial red berries and a bow are a perfect accompaniment.

Robert Gray

EVERGREEN WREATHS

Three evergreen wreaths, 8, 10, and 12 inches round, are beautifully filled out by winter ivy that has been generously wrapped around each wreath to create a lush green backdrop for clusters of green limes. Fresh fruit should be glued to the wreath to avoid damaging the surface of the fruit. The display's success is due to the vertical arrangement of the wreaths, which are anchored by wire to a wide green velvet ribbon, headed by a velvet bow.

David Arky

Another beautiful, natural wreath idea is made by inserting dried flowers—baby's breath, statice, roses, and mallow—directly into an evergreen wreath. The addition of a gilt or pastel bow makes a wreath that it ideal for interior decoration. Place it over a mantelpiece or in an entry area to add a

David Arky

fragrant, woodsy appeal to any holiday decor. This wreath becomes a year-round pleasure as it dries: Its color changes from green to burnished copper while its scent becomes more subtle. Wreaths that you wish to preserve by drying should be placed away from direct sunlight in a dry, protected location.

Robert Gray

Outdoor wreaths lend themselves to very bold touches. This huge wreath is full of twinkling electric lights, and dozens of small artificial birds are fastened to its branches. A very dramatic red bow provides a swath of Christmas color.

A simple evergreen wreath placed in a window is given a special interest as it is placed over a window box filled with foil-wrapped presents.

Robert Gray

Robert Gray

The evergreen wreath hanging on this family's door is echoed by matching evergreen wreaths, in miniature, hanging in all the house's windows. A long, swagging rope of evergreen boughs along the front fence creates a picture of this home that is symmetrical, understated, and reflecting great style.

When you are attaching greens to a doorway or mantel, consider inserting a small staple where you need anchorage, then wiring the greens to the staple, not to the door. This will leave only a tiny mar in the door, and is quite strong. It is also possible to insert a staple into the top width of the door and hang clear fisherman's line from it to hold wreaths and swagging, avoiding any visible marks.

EVERGREEN WREATHS

The red-bowed wreath in this picture is only part of a very fanciful entry design. Again, evergreen roping is used. This time it follows the shape of the doorway, and has a sprinkling of tiny electric lights. Wonderful holiday cherubs, which seem to float above the entrance, welcome visitors.

Robert Gray

Vine, Everlasting, and Cone Wreaths

For locations throughout the home, and as gifts that will provide years of pleasure to the recipient, vine-based wreaths are a perfect choice. In addition, vine wreaths are appropriate year round—simply replace a Christmas bow with seasonal flowers or other ornaments of your choice.

The basic structure of this wreath is twisted vine—grape, virginia creeper, or honeysuckle. These provide a textured, strong, and lasting shape and support for any number of embellishments. Vine wreaths are now widely available through nurseries and Christmas specialty stores during the holiday season. If you prefer to make your own vine wreath, the technique is a simple one.

To make a grapevine wreath, cut 3-foot lengths of grape vine. If you have an arbor, cut your vines once

the weather has become cold and the vines are dormant. You will need between 3 and 6 lengths, depending on the bulk of wreath you want to make. Soak the vines in hot water until they are pliable, then form them into the circle size desired, securing the circumference with a small piece of florist wire; continue winding and tucking the remaining vine from that length. Follow with a second or third length, using the same technique and wrapping each around those already shaped. Secure all beginning and end points of the circles with florist wire. If your vines are short, make 3 to 10 circles of one vine each, stack them, and tie together by winding a ribbon or rope around the stack.

CHRISTMAS WREATHS

Homemade wreaths often have a more natural, woodland appeal when they are made of wild vines from regional plants. These wreaths often are more meaningful to friends and family. To make wreaths from wild vines, trim 4 vines (3 to 6 feet in length) of most of their leaves. Tie them together at one end with a string of florist wire, then twist them to form a circle, circling twice, if your vines are very long. Secure the ends by tucking them back into the circle as you go. Tie 4 more vines together in the same manner, tucking the beginning end around the back of the circle that you have already made. Wrap these vines around your circle, fastening the ends by tucking them into the wreath as you go. Fresh vines are very pliable, so shape them by gently pulling and adjusting individual strands. Weight the wreath under a heavy book overnight to dry it out and to help it "remember" its shape.

VINE, EVERLASTING, AND CONE WREATHS

Robert Gray

David Arky

If you would like to make a heart-shaped wild vine wreath, follow the procedure on page 30. When you have the base circle you want, bend it into a heart shape, then wrap the top layer of vines around that shape. Some of the vines will break at the base of the heart and at its dip, but most are pliable enough to remain intertwined. Weight the heart-shaped vines overnight, then decorate with ribbon, or, as illustrated here, dried hydrangea, and a tiny fabric bird glued into a real bird's nest (found, perhaps, on a family hike), which has been wired to the base of the wreath.

David Arky

The dense, knotted circle of a vine wreath will anchor dried flowers, spices, herbs, and other branches with no additional tying or gluing. Tucked into the branches of this Mexican spice wreath are various hot peppers and bay leaves. The wreath is wrapped with a narrow gilt ribbon, onto which is tied bunches of stick cinnamon. This sort of wreath, beautiful as well as usable, makes a wonderful gift wreath for the great cook among your friends.

CHRISTMAS WREATHS

Baby's breath, eucalyptus leaves, purple statice, and fresh roses make a very romantic statement in this wreath. Simply tuck these elements into a vine wreath and wire any protruding eucalyptus branches down to the wreath. The addition of an antique porcelain doll resting on the branches adds nostalgia to the romance—a lovely wreath for a Victorian setting.

Robert Gray

Robert Gray

Dried roses, tucked into a vine wreath that is loaded with soft-hued dried herbs and grasses, create an elegant look. Here, the small cupid-like cherub tied in pastel ribbon results in a wreath that carries itself beautifully from Christmastime through Valentine's day.

CHRISTMAS WREATHS

A woodland look is achieved here with a vine wreath filled with dried grasses, which holds a small bird's nest into which is tucked a ceramic bird.

Robert Gray

Robert Gray

Vine-based wreaths that "escape" from the con-
fines of their circular structure can achieve a highly
original look. This circle of pale vines has an
exuberant topping of red dried everlastings—
cockscomb, spike, sumac—that are wired to the vine
wreath in a sunburst fashion, emanating from the
top center of the wreath. The deep red tones of the
plants are lovely against the deep green sprigs of ivy
that have been inserted along the top curve of the
pale vines.

37

Robert Gray

The unusual color of this wreath is a combination of mallow, rosy statice, eucalyptus leaves, and a generous amount of dried dusty miller inserted into a vine wreath. The wonderful, rangy effect is a result of non-conforming grey branches. A tousled, exotic look results.

Another wreath's success is owed to the original placement of everlastings in a eucalyptus base. Baby's breath, purple statice, and red roses are tucked into the eucalyptus, which has been tied to a wire base. The statice and roses have been symmetrically placed on what appears to be a jumble of baby's breath.

Robert Gray

A vine wreath that is as heavy with grasses and flowers as this one is requires extra "building." Begin by inserting a heavy layer of dried grasses into the vine branches. The vines themselves should become almost invisible. Tie this layer of grasses down by wrapping the entire wreath with pale thread, circling it twice. Use your least interesting grasses and flowers for this base, as they are really just creating a backdrop. Now insert your finer grasses, herbs, and strawflowers. The dense infrastructure will anchor them securely and the effect will be lush yet feathery. The addition of a beautiful bow (change it as the colors of the seasons change), creates a wreath that will be cherished throughout the year.

Dried everlasting wreaths can give many years of pleasure if cared for properly. As with dried evergreen wreaths, these should be hung in a dry, low-traffic location, away from direct sunlight. For seasonal storage, wrap them in white tissue, box and store in a cool, dry location, secure from the interest of mice and squirrels.

Bo Parker

42

VINE, EVERLASTING, AND CONE WREATHS

Pinecone wreaths are classic, enduring Christmas decorations. The intricate beauty and infinite variety of the cones need no additional adornment. With careful construction and storage, these wreaths are treasures that will last for many years. To make your own, you will need to collect pinecones of assorted sizes—at least two dozen of each of the varieties you would like to use. You will also need to purchase a 6-, 8-, or 10-inch wire wreath form at a nursery or variety store to use as a base for the wreath. Begin by soaking the pinecones in warm water until their "petals" close. Prop up your wire form so that it is parallel with your work table, about 2 inches above the surface, then place the closed cones very snugly inside the circles of the wreath. It is best to begin with large cones and fill in with smaller ones. As the cones dry out, their petals open, interlocking them with the wire frame and with each other. Any additional decorative cones or ribbon should be wired to the wreath after the cones have completely opened and set.

Novelty Wreaths

Classic evergreen, vine, everlasting, and pinecone wreaths represent only some of the creative choices available to the Christmas artist. Materials for holiday wreaths are as varied as the locations in which you can display them. Use your sense of whimsy when designing the special touches for these wreaths; and let your imagination reign when placing them in your home. These wreaths will add novel charm over a children's table, create a focal point of holiday spirit at the head of the stairs, or bring coziness to a family room.

Fabric and crafts shops feature many kinds of "base" wreaths on which to build very personalized ones. In addition to vine and wire forms, rounded, pale straw-wreath forms are widely available. Use these 10-inch bases to create the wreaths illustrated on the next two pages.

NOVELTY WREATHS

David Arky

   This wreath is made of long, dried pine needles
that are laid against a straw base and then secured
by wrapping matching thread around the circle.
Cover the wreath twice in this fashion, so that the
needles are dense enough to completely cover the
straw. Plaid fabric ribbon is then wound around the
wreath and tied in a bow at the base. Glue small
pieces of cardboard along the base of the wreath
with white glue. To these pieces, glue a variety of
tiny wooden buildings and animals, creating a small
country scene. The addition of baby's breath,
lightly glued between the buildings, gives the illu-
sion of foliage in your "town."

David Arky

The light, feathery appearance of this wreath is provided by straw that is used for packing—the sort that you have probably discarded time and again. The next time a package arrives filled with straw, set some aside to create this cheerful wreath. Once again, use a straw wreath base. Gently pull the packing straw apart so that it is loosely meshed together, then wrap it around the base until the entire wreath is lightly covered with loose straw. Tie fabric ribbon in bows around five candy canes. Using pale thread, tie these at even intervals around the straw, tying the thread around the back of the wreath base. This thread holds both the candy canes and the straw in place on the wreath.

Robert Gray

A wire wreath base lends itself to countless unusual applications. This charming eucalyptus wreath uses a wire frame as its base. Small bunches of baby's breath are tied at intervals to the eucalyptus, which in turn is tied to a wire wreath base with florist wire. A long strand of ½-inch pastel ribbon is then tied at the top of the wreath. The final effect is very feminine and unique—certainly a genteel holiday creation.

47

CHRISTMAS WREATHS

A wildly curling wreath of streamers is a festive addition to any holiday decor. Its base is a wire wreath frame, which is decorated with three or four packages of muticolored streamers. To assemble this wreath, lightly cover the wire frame with white glue. Gently unravel a two-streamer width of paper streamers, pulling them from inside the streamer tube, being careful not to separate the curls. Loosely wrap these lengths around the wire frame, front and back. Randomly "spot" this first layer of streamers with white glue, then continue to wrap additional streamers around the wreath. No additional glue will be necessary, as the curling streamers will hold each other in place. Continue, alternating colors, until you have a full, wildly curling effect. Loosely tie the wreath in four places with bright, paper curling ribbon for extra texture and interest.

NOVELTY WREATHS

49

David Arky

50

NOVELTY WREATHS

Intricate collections of tiny treasures are fascinating for young and old alike. The circle of a wreath provides all the visual organization necessary to create a masterpiece of miniatures. The wreath pictured is made of small dimestore-quality toys, blocks, and ornaments, all of which are given new elegance with gold spray paint. Small plastic fruits, sewing notions, and old puzzle and boardgame pieces, have an amazing new decorative life when ribboned and painted.

This wreath is built in three stages. First, glue a collection of unpainted, flat-sided objects to a wire wreath frame, using gluing cement. Once the cement has dried, place a few objects around the wreath base. Second, lightly spray paint the small objects you have chosen with gold paint, taking care to rotate them so that all sides are painted. Third, when the wreath base-paint and the objects are dry, glue the small treasures to the base. Wait for that cement to set, and then very lightly spray the entire wreath with gold paint. For the final touch, tie small, gilt fabric bows directly to any part of the wreath base that remains exposed in the front of the wreath. This is a most delicate creation, and should be placed out of reach of small, fascinated hands.

David Arky

52

NOVELTY WREATHS

Burlap fabric makes a wonderful wreath material. These two small wreaths—fine on a doll's house, as napkin rings, or on a tree—are plush and charming. They are made from 8-foot lengths of unwashed burlap, cut 2½-inches wide, and pieces of fine florist wire. Fray the straight strips of burlap by pulling out the long burlap threads from both long sides of the fabric length until you have strips with ¾-inch intact centers, and ¾-inch fraying on either side. Use your florist wire as a needle, and sew a running stitch down the center of the length, stitching at ¼-inch intervals. When you are finished, the burlap will be tightly gathered. Twist the ends of the wire together to make a small circle, snipping off excess wire. Trim the tiny wreath with small plaid bows, which are secured to the wreath with burlap thread. They can be further decorated with glued-on sprigs of holly, baby's breath, and tiny ornaments.

Robert Gray

CHRISTMAS CENTERPIECES

The spirit of Christmas continues throughout the house, manifest in the tree decorated with the family's ornaments, swags of spruce and fir, candlelight and Christmas cookies. Christmas centerpieces, as their name implies, are a focal point in this holiday array, whether on a table set for Christmas dinner, a buffet, or a mantelpiece.

The Christmas season, with its festive nature and generous tradition, affords the centerpiece designer dozens of styles and materials to choose from when creating. Greens, flowers, fruit, candles, cookies, mementos and baubles create a huge reservoir of possibilities for the creation of centerpieces.

Begin at the Beginning

It is very important to begin this creative process by taking a look at your home's special style, or that of the friend for whom you will be designing a gift. Is it countrified, urban, Victorian, eclectic? Are you making a centerpiece for a special place in your home such as the Christmas table? If you are making a gift, and are unsure of style and placement, stay with designs that are smaller in size and traditional in design—arrangements of flowers, baskets of greens.

The second step is to assemble all your available materials for making centerpieces. Take stock of what you might need in the way of basic florist's supplies: garden shears, florist wire, oasis (that green, water-absorbing foam for flower arranging), and other anchoring devices. Look next at your raw materials: holly, baby's breath, fir and pine boughs, pinecones. Having all of these items in your home "stock" will prepare you for all sorts of projects. Finally, assemble your assorted containers and embellishments. This includes assorted baskets, bowls of glass, silver, and pottery, as well as bows and ribbons, special Christmas mementos, ornaments, and small Christmas treasures. (This is the right time to assemble candlesticks and prospective linens if you are designing for yourself.)

You are now ready to begin. Let the variety of greens, ribbons, and embellishments work together with your interpretation of your family or friend's style to inspire a memorable Christmas centerpiece.

Tony Cenicola

Flowers, Greens, and Fruit

Holly, pine boughs, and pinecones are classic Christmas favorites. They instill a holiday look that is beautifully expanded upon with the addition of the whites and reds of poinsettia, chrysanthemum, carnations, and baby's breath.

Tony Cenicola

Pictured is a centerpiece whose country look is civilized enough to be carried from an entry hall to the Christmas table. Placed in a rustic willow basket is a small water dish that holds a square piece of oasis, into which has been inserted pine and fir branches, baby's breath, and pinecones that have strands of florist wire wound around their bases, leaving a 6- to 8-inch length of wire to insert into the oasis base. An arrangement as simple as this lends itself to many flourishes—the addition of small real, or artificial flowers, small ornaments, a plaid or gilt bow, a fabric bird, or the addition of paper doilies inserted around the rim of the basket before arranging the greens.

FLOWERS, GREENS, AND FRUIT

A more lavish presentation of many of the same
elements is represented with this centerpiece exam-
ple. It is built in the same way as the previous one,
but credits its look to a greater array of flowers
placed in a higher basket, which is studded with
numerous wispy branches of holiday berries. The
flowers, greens, and branches are all artificial—the
natural, lush appearance certainly is not.

John Deane

CHRISTMAS CENTERPIECES

Fine artificial flowers serve a great purpose during the Christmas season. They provide a variety not dependent on seasonal availability, and, with care, will provide years of pleasure. The simple addition of fabric poinsettias to a bowl of loosely placed pine branches is an elegant, contemporary touch.

John Deane

A very structured arrangement in the Japanese style is easiest to achieve through the use of artificial flowers. The starry look of the chrysanthemums and the underpinnnings of holly give this arrangement a holiday air. Its open look makes it a perfect choice as a table centerpiece—beautiful, yet uninhibiting to table views and conversation. As with natural flower arrangements, these stems are anchored in oasis, but, of course, are to remain dry and unwatered.

John Deane

Robert Gray

Fruit is a glorious, bounteous choice as the main element in a Christmas centerpiece. The glowing reds and greens of apples, the frosty purple of grapes, and the brown-skinned pears look beautiful in combination with each other, and with holiday greenery. Unblemished fresh fruit is most classically arranged in a pyramid shape. This photograph shows a gorgeous presentation of assorted fruit arranged in a compote, and to achieve height, the arrangement is crowned by a pineapple, the colonial symbol of hospitality. The height is softened by the careful arrangement of fir branches around the base, which is studded by additional fruit and small statuary.

Robert Gray

A more horizontal arrangement of fruit makes a
perfect setting for the seasonal wassail bowl. The
bowl is elevated on a circular platter, slightly larger
than the bowl itself. The platter is hidden by pine
boughs; the base of the bowl is rimmed by fruit,
creating a low, terraced effect on the table. A swirl of
pine boughs, set directly on the tabletop and pep-
pered with fruit and berries, completes a centerpiece that is relaxed yet rich in texture and color.

Setting a Christmas Stage

A very creative, personal approach to the creation of Christmas centerpieces is a theatrical approach. That is, to use your design and its location to build a mood, evoke a memory, create a tradition. The personalized adornments of a miniature Christmas tree, the child's touch in the building of a gingerbread house, a thoughtfully arranged collection of

Bo Parker

beloved Christmas memorabilia, are all parts of this evocative look. The careful arrangement of three glass bowls, each holding a single floating gardenia on a circle of mirrored glass that is scattered with glass balls, makes a very individual centerpiece; its snowy flowers and silvery reflections are appropriate for this season.

CHRISTMAS CENTERPIECES

A miniature Christmas tree is certainly one of the most charming centerpieces you could choose for your home. The tree itself can be either a miniature pine, or a well-shaped conical juniper bush—both are widely available through florists and nurseries. If the tree is to be used on a dining table, the height should not exceed 18 inches from trunk base to top, and the tree should be cut from its root ball; insert its trunk in a low, heavy water dish containing a heavy, floral anchoring stand. The water dish can then be camouflaged by pinecones, a loose wrapping of lace, or tiny toys and gifts. Decorate the tree with tiny ornaments, ribbons, strings of seed pearls, and narrow gold roping. Continue the magical look upward—tie golden stars from the chandelier above with gold thread and space them randomly above the tree.

Robert Gray

SETTING A CHRISTMAS STAGE

Making a gingerbread house is a holiday tradition for many families. Use this marvelous sculpture as a centerpiece this holiday season. The building of this fantasy house is easier than it appears—particularily since hard, decorative icing hides a multitude of errors. First, construct a suitable house frame from cardboard—four sides and a pitched roof. Next, prepare a double batch of gingerbread dough, using your favorite recipe. Then, using your cardboard sides and roof as your template, roll and cut the dough, baking it according to directions. Cool on wire racks and piece together the house using a hard, white icing as your "glue." Make the icing by combining enough stiffly beaten egg whites with powdered sugar to make it stiff enough to hold its shape, yet fluid enough to feed through a pastry tube. When the sides and roof of the gingerbread house have hardened into position, embellish the façade with piped, swirling icing, using the icing again as glue to attach numerous sugarplums.

Robert Gray

Finally, a sweet collection of foil-covered Santas makes a very lustrous, witty centerpiece. There is no construction here—this is stage-setting at its best— a beautiful result with very little effort. Interesting placement of the figures (here, on a white cloth), along with balls of foil candies, is all that is necessary. Foil-wrapped Christmas candies look beautiful heaped in silver bowls, and just a few Santas among pairs of tall silver candlesticks, have a decidedly jolly look.